Ghost S

of

Leicestershire

by

ANGELA CUTTING

ANDERSON BLABY

First published 1982
Revised 1990

Illustration of the
Blue Boar Inn
by
Brian Hollingshead

Other illustrations by Robert Duncan

ISBN 0 907917 00 3

Anderson Publications
The Fairway, Blaby, Leicester
Printed by A.B. Printers Ltd, Leicester

Contents

From ghoulies and ghosties and long leggety beasties
And things that go bump in the night,
Good Lord, deliver us!

Old Scottish Prayer

Foreword

Tales of hauntings and strange phenomena have terrified and fascinated people for centuries. Indeed an unquestioning belief in ghosts and spirits seems to have been perfectly natural until about one hundred years ago. So much so that one of the local Mediaeval Gilds *[sic]* had a regulation forbidding members of the Watch from conjuring up spirits during their night duty, which they were apt to do to wile away the time!

I have always had a great fascination myself for ghost stories and have collected accounts of local hauntings. In 1977, as a Leicester City Guide, I decided to prepare a tour of local 'haunts' for inclusion in the programme of guided walks which is held each year. The resulting Leicester Ghost Walk has since proved to be so popular that it is repeated every year at Walpurgis Night, Halloween, and Christmas.

This book was written after I had received many requests to put the stories down on paper. Some of the accounts are from the past, found in old newspaper articles, several are almost local legends, whilst others are more recent reports which have been recounted to me by the witnesses. My aim has not been a learned treatise on ghosts, but to make available the stories of various hauntings and to preserve them, as part of the rich folklore of the city and county.

To all those who have given me their accounts and stories and who have kindly allowed me to include them in this book, I would like to express my sincere thanks.

Angela M Cutting

Leicester
1982

The old
Blue Boar Inn
Leicester

A Hoard of Gold

There are many legends surrounding the life of Richard III, some of which are connected with Leicester. One in particular concerns the Blue Boar Inn which used to stand on the corner of Blue Boar Lane and Highcross Street. The original name of the inn was the 'White Boar', and it was here that Richard spent the night on the eve of his death at the Battle of Bosworth in 1485.

It is said that Richard III always took his own bed when he was on the road, and it was set up in the Inn on the night of his stay. The bed was left at the Inn and never claimed, for Richard was killed the following day at Bosworth Field. The White Boar was Richard's badge, so when the landlord of the inn heard the news of the King's defeat, he cleverly repainted his inn sign blue — the blue boar was the badge of one of Henry VII's supporters, the Earl of Oxford. So, the inn became known thereafter as the Blue Boar.

Apparently the famous bed remained at the Inn for two hundred years or more because it is further rumoured that at the beginning of the seventeenth century the landlord of the Blue Boar found a hoard of gold hidden inside the bed. The landlord died soon after this, but his widow, Agnes Clarke, carried on running the Inn. Rumours about the gold spread, and on 3rd February, 1605 Agnes caught some men trying to steal moneybags from her room. One of the men, Edward Bradshaw, bundled Agnes onto the bed and stifled her cries by thrusting the material of her gown down her throat. Agnes choked to death and the men fled the scene. However, the murderers were caught and found guilty, Bradshaw was hanged, Thomas Harrison, his accomplice, was sent to prison, and a maid at the inn who had plotted the theft with the two men was burnt at the stake in Gallowtree Gate.

It appears that the spirit of Agnes Clarke was not appeased by the executions as her ghost haunted the Inn until it was pulled down, and was known as the White Lady. When a new Blue Boar was built in 1836 in Southgate Street, the ghost of the 'White Lady' was said to have moved there too!

Are You There Harry Staines

The landlord of the pub in Churchgate, Leicester, concerned with this strange story, and his wife had been living at the premises for about six months when they began to realise that something weird was happening in the public rooms as well as their own living quarters on the first floor.

Glasses jumped off tables into the air; a sheet disappeared without trace from one of the beds and a figure seen going into a room one evening by the bar staff just seemed to disappear. The landlord's cat also seemed to sense that something was wrong — he would often be peacefully asleep in the flat, and then for no apparent reason, he would suddenly leap into the air, hair on end, and run out of the room in a very nervous state.

The landlord's wife occasionally felt something tap her on the shoulder when she was quite alone. The landlord told me that when he went up the stairs leading to his flat, he usually felt that he was being followed, although no one could be seen. They both said that they could definitely sense when the ghost was around.

One Sunday morning a visitor in the flat was looking out of the window, gazing at the building opposite, when he saw reflected in one of its windows, what seemed to be a figure moving about in the floor above the flat. This floor was not used and was closed off at the time. But, on investigation no one was discovered.

The ghost was only seen on one occasion. The landlord was working behind the bar in the evening, when he saw what he describes as a 'white, shapeless mist' float past him and then disappear through the closed door leading into the cellar.

Intrigued by the ghostly activity on the premises, the landlord's wife decided to do some research into the pub's history to see if anyone had passed away on the premises. She found out that a former landlord, Harry Staines, had died there, but she could not discover how his death had occured. About a year later, an unexpected letter arrived at the pub from a medium in Lancashire, in which he claimed to have been contacted by the spirit of Harry Staines during a seance. This spirit had told the medium his name, that he had been the landlord of the pub, and that he had died in October 1896, aged 29, when he fell down the steps leading to the cellar. This letter confirmed the landlord's own feelings about the ghost, and was considered genuine, for how else could the medium have found out.

The Man in the Gallery

Most theatres are said to be haunted and there are some well-known stories. In fact, many actors and theatre staff believe that it is a sign that a play will go well when the ghost appears in the theatre on the first night of a production, or during rehearsals.

Leicester's Haymarket Theatre is no exception and there are two stories associated with it. The first ghost apparently appeared to one of the backstage staff during the rehearsal for a musical. A young boy dressed in an old fashioned type of sailor suit was seen loitering near the props. He was not supposed to be there, so was told to go away. He did — vanishing into thin air!

This boy has been seen on several occasions. During a performance of *Godspell* at the Theatre one of the box office staff saw a small arm and hand appear round a door, and thinking it was one of the many young children taking part in the production, immediately went to investigate, but no one was there.

In 1981 the Theatre produced Shakespeare's *Hamlet,* and one day the actress playing Ophelia saw a young boy standing at the side of the stage. She started to walk towards him intending to find out who he was, when the figure just disappeared.

There have been other reports of this boy being seen at the Theatre, and it is thought he may have some connection with the Victorian buildings which used to stand on the site.

The second story was reported by a musician who has worked at the Theatre as a drummer. At the commencement of intervals in the performance, the musicians carefully covered their instruments and left the orchestra pit. The entrance gate was closed and securely locked behind them. On occasions, when musicians returned in readiness for the programme to continue, a very different scene met their eyes. Instruments were knocked over, the music sheets and stands were strewn about the floor, and everything was in a mess. After making enquiries, it was discovered that no one could have entered the pit without the keys, which were in the possession of one of the musicians. Perhaps it was the mischievous work of the boy in the sailor suit!

The old Palace Theatre which used to stand in Belgrave Gate, nearly opposite the position occupied by the Haymarket Theatre, also had its own ghost. One night the manager was in the stalls checking that all patrons had left before locking up for the night, when he looked up and saw the figure of a shabbily dressed old man walking towards the exit from the gallery. The manager was curious and went upstairs to investigate but on arriving at the gallery the man had disappeared. The next day he spoke of the incident to one of the usherettes, thinking that she had not made sure that the gallery was empty before leaving. The usherette denied that she had been careless, adding that the mysterious figure sounded like one she herself had seen. On at least two previous occasions when she had approached the old man to speak to him, he vanished before her eyes.

The ghost is said to be very like an old tramp who was found dead in the entrance hall of the Floral Hall Cinema, next door to the theatre.

The Grey Lady of Swithland

The legend which tells of a ghost known as the *Grey Lady of Swithland* goes back to the first half of the nineteenth-century, and concerns the tragic death of a young lady at Swithland's old Rectory.

The Rector of that time had gone away with his family, leaving the house in the care of the butler, a man called Parker. It seems that Parker was subject to occasional mad fits and while the family was away managed to force his way into the cellar and drank some of the wine kept there.

The Rector's twenty year old daughter returned home before the rest of the family and finding the butler drunk, retired to bed and, feeling rather uneasy, locked her bedroom door. At about midnight Parker, by now even more intoxicated, broke into the pretty young girl's bedroom with a rope in his hand and, after a struggle, hanged her from the top of her own four-poster bed. When he had recovered his senses he realised with horror the terrible deed he had committed and was so struck with remorse that he cut his own throat with a carving knife.

After the murder, and for the next hundred years until the Rectory was demolished, strange screams and wails could sometimes be heard in the village at night, and the ghosts of both the butler and the Lady were seen. The Lady appeared in a beautiful grey brocade dress and her murderer with blood pouring from his throat, crying out with anguish.

It has also been reported that the Grey Lady was seen in the church porch while a service was in progress, and that she also appeared at garden parties when the old Rectory was still standing.

After the demolition of the old Rectory, the Grey Lady was seen walking away from the site of her former home towards Swithland Church, her head bowed and carrying a stone slab. The significance of this short walk taken in such a manner is not known, but the Grey Lady has not been seen since.

Footsteps in Friar Lane

In 1978 one of the Ghost Walks organised by the Leicester Information Bureau was held on Halloween, 31st October. The tour included a property in Friar Lane and, as the guide related the following incident to her party, she noted that one of the ladies was particularly attentive.

In Friar Lane, one of the oldest parts of Leicester, one haunting originally dates back to the 1820s when an invisible person could be heard walking about with loud footsteps in one of the houses. A hundred years later the house had been converted into offices and the ghost was heard again.

One evening a girl was working late in a ground floor office in the company of a friend who was waiting for her. The building was completely empty but for the two girls. Suddenly, they heard heavy footsteps coming from the rooms upstairs, and then come slowly down the stairs. The girls naturally took fright and ran outside, only to realise that all the lights were still on. One of the girls reluctantly went back to switch them off and lock up the building. She was very relieved to see or hear nothing on her return.

The following day, talking about her experiences to her colleagues the girl was surprised to hear that the typists who worked upstairs had previously heard strange noises as well, and that doors used to open and close for no apparent reason. At the time it was thought that the building was haunted by a man who had hanged himself in a small room upstairs. The man had failed in business whilst living in the house.

The guide paused at this point and the attentive lady in the party confirmed that the story was authentic — in her youth she had been that frightened typist!

A second haunting which took place in Friar Lane also dates back to the last century. A young boy who regularly walked along Friar Lane to St. Mary de Castro Church was frequently followed at night by footsteps. They would begin approximately in the middle of Friar Lane and always ended in front of the church.

The boy only saw something on one occasion, a Midsummer's Eve. Then, as well as hearing the footsteps, he saw a shadow moving along the ground beside him. The shadow was that of a headless man with a humped back. It followed the boy until he reached St. Mary's church doorway when it passed through the closed, heavy wooden door.

The Cloaked Figure

A lady who was in Guildhall Lane one afternoon in 1977, stopped to look into a shop window at the corner of Loseby Lane. Suddenly she became aware that someone was behind her and, on glancing round, was startled by the vision of an exceptionally tall man brushing past her. She could not see the man's face as it was hidden beneath a dark, wide-brimmed hat, but she did notice that he was wearing a long, old fashioned, dark coloured cloak or cape, not used nowadays. After turning back to the window, she became curious about the strange-looking figure and took a second glance towards the place where she expected to see the man but was very surprised to find that he had apparently disappeared. Thinking about the incident afterwards, the lady realised that the figure had made no noise whatsoever, not even the sound of footsteps.

At least two other people are known to have seen the same figure in the neighbourhood of Guildhall Lane and both have described the man as wearing a long, dark coat or cloak and a large hat. Both also noticed the absence of any footsteps. The most recently known sighting happened at the beginning of 1980. A man was walking along Guildhall Lane late one evening and saw a strange figure walking towards him. The figure turned off the pavement and as it began to cross the road, faded away.

Licensed to Sell Spirits

A public house in King Richards Road, Leicester, was haunted by a former landlady. Some years previous one of the former tenants, an elderly lady, Mrs Smith was moved out by the brewery to enable them to modernise the property. This was against Mrs Smith's wishes and she threatened that, in due course, she would come back and haunt the premises!

It seems that she got her wish. A later landlord's wife once saw the ghostly figure of an old woman in an orange dress, in her bedroom. When she described the appearance of the figure to an old customer it tallied exactly with that of Mrs Smith.

The Centre Hotel in Humberstone Gate stands on the site of the former Freeman, Hardy and Willis shoe factory. During the war the factory was bombed, killing the night watchman. Later it is said that his ghost haunted the site during the construction there of a new building.

One day some of the builders were working on an upper floor when they saw a man go out of a door on one side of the room. They thought it was just another workman until a few seconds later when they saw the figure of the same man return through an unconnected door on the opposite side of the room, and then finally disappear.

A discotheque in Churchgate is reputedly haunted by the ghost of a small girl. Indeed, this building has been the scene of several strange events. A particular spare room upstairs is supposed to be haunted and at one time staff disliked going into it after dark. The room was tastefully decorated and illuminated by an attractive chandelier. One evening a young female assistant was told to go upstairs to fetch an article from this room. She reluctantly obeyed, and on reaching the upper landing, opened the door into the room and turned on the lights. Looking in she was terrified to see what she afterwards described as a face suddenly materialise among the glass pendants of the light fitting.

Five to Four Fred

One of the most well-known haunted pubs in Leicestershire is perhaps the Belper Arms at Newton Burgoland, a few miles west of Ibstock. The oldest part of the pub was built about 700 years ago, originally as a cottage for the masons working nearby at Swepstone Church. When it later became the local hostelry, it was called The Shepherd and Shepherdess; it was renamed the Belper Arms after the pub's seventeenth-century owner, the Earl of Belper.

This 12th century inn is haunted by a ghost nick-named 'Five to Four Fred' because of its habit of making its presence felt at this particular time, either in the morning or afternoon. Whilst the ghost has never been seen, it has definitely been felt in more ways than one! Fred seems to have a strong preference to women as they are liable to feel him gently stroking their faces, or slapping and pinching their bottoms! Men, on the other hand, feel hands pressing over their mouths and they are unable to breathe until they go outside the pub. A sudden distinct drop in temperature is usually the first sign of the ghost's presence.

The ghost seems to have made its first appearance some years ago when a former landlord took over the pub and had an old staircase removed from the original part of the building. While they were in bed one night the wife and daughter of the landlord felt something stroke their faces, as well as a sensation which they later described as akin to a cat walking across the bed. On another occasion a friend stayed overnight at the pub and, as the bedrooms were full, slept on the bar floor. After being asleep for some time he was awakened by intense cold and what can only be described as the sensation of being suffocated. There was however no one else present in the bar.

Fred does not seem to restrict his activities solely to human beings. Other odd things have happened. A kettle has suddenly jumped into the air and glasses and pots have fallen from their shelves onto the floor without a sound.

The Sergeant and the Tomb

In the churchyard of St Mary's Church at Hinckley is a tomb, called by local legend the 'Bloody Tomb' because of the strange drops of red liquid which appear on the tombstone every year in April.

The story which surrounds this mystery dates back to the eighteenth-century when a young local man was killed in the market place. Richard Smith, a saddler in Hinckley, aged twenty, saw a crowd of people in the market place on 12th April, 1727. A recruiting sergeant stood in the midst of the crowd regaling them with frightening stories about the future that awaited themselves and their families if James Stuart came to the throne. The townspeople seemed cowed and silent, but Richard was made of sterner stuff and called out a joke which made everyone in the crowd laugh.

The sergeant was furious, taking great exception to a joke made at his expense. In a rage he hurled himself towards Richard driving his halberd through Smith's chest, killing him. The sergeant promptly disappeared and, apparently, was never captured.

The unfortunate victim was buried in St. Mary's churchyard, and the following inscription was put on his tombstone:

A fatal halberd then his body slew,
The murdering hand God's vengeance will pursue
From earthly shades though Justice took her flight
Shall not the Judge of all the world do right
Each age and sex his innocence bemoans
And with sad sighs lament his dying groans.

According to tradition drops of a liquid which resembles blood appear on the tombstone each April. The contemporary explanation by local people was that the tomb was crying tears of blood because the recruiting sergeant had escaped justice.

Tea on the Lawn

It happened in 1972; not so much a ghost story, but more of a glimpse back in time. It was related to me as follows.

'A few years ago my daughter who was then fifteen years old, her friend and myself explored the deserted old manor house in Canal Street, Thurmaston. It used to be occupied by an old lady from a very well known family, who eventually finished up living in one room until she died. She had often told me how wonderful it was in the old days.

'There was a gate through which we could enter the front drive and, from there into the terribly overgrown garden. Another gate led from the orchard through an enormous old greenhouse at the back. The garden was a complete wilderness, right up to the doors at the back of the house. We crept in the back way, and I was immediately conscious of a strange feeling. It was weird but not unpleasant. My daughter and her friend went round to the doors at the back, where at one time there must have been a lawn. I walked round the other way. A few moments later, the two girls came rushing up to me and said that, as they came through the trees, they saw a perfect lawn where a young man and two young ladies were sitting having tea on a white tablecloth, spread over the grass. The man was wearing light summer clothing and a straw hat; the two girls were in very old fashioned dresses. As my daughter and her friend watched from behind the overgrown bushes the group got up from the lawn and walked to the side gate laughing and talking as they went.

'The gate is a good distance from the road, so we all ran out along the drive, into the road expecting to see the man and the girls. But when we arrived there, we could see nothing. No cars or people, just nothing. If they had been real we would have caught them up anyway, before they reached the main gate! We went back and entered the empty house. There was no lawn, and no people. The incident shook us quite a lot.'

Unfortunately, the old house has now been demolished.

Uninvited Guests

Hauntings of dwellings are certainly not limited to old ancestral stately homes, or to very ancient buildings. Many ordinary semi-detached and terraced houses have had their fair share of ghosts too! This section deals with a few homes in Leicester which have been haunted.

The first story concerns a house in Oak Street, which had once been a smithy, and where it is reported that one of the previous occupants murdered his wife. Some years later after the house had changed hands a couple were in bed one night, when the woman suddenly went stiff with fright and fainted. When finally brought round she was too scared to say what was wrong, but would not stay in the house a moment longer. Apparently, she ran out of the house in her night clothes and drove off to spend the night elsewhere. Later she explained that she had been woken up in the night and saw a woman dressed in Victorian clothes standing at the foot of the bed, pointing a finger at her and wearing a particularly malevolent expression.

The second case is about a house which seems to have been haunted by water! The house was situated in Bell Lane and at the time of the story, 1933, was occupied by a couple and their thirteen year old daughter. Water suddenly began to pour out of the walls in spurts and run down to the floor. Despite investigations by workmen from the water department, no trace of any dampness could ever be found under the floor, and amazingly the wall-paper was never damaged in any way. The workmen could find no reason for the sudden jets of water appearing, and it was declared a complete mystery. A few weeks later the same thing happened, and again no trace could be found of the cause. At the time, it was thought that the phenomena may have been caused by a poltergeist triggered off by the presence of the adolescent daughter.

My own grandparents had a strange experience when they were living in a house in Brandon Street, Leicester. The house had been formerly owned by an elderly lady and my grandparents moved into the house after her death. The woman's daughter lived in the house next door.

One night while they were in bed, my grandmother heard a noise downstairs and mentioned it to my grandfather. He replied that it was nothing and told her to go back to sleep. However, they then heard the sound of footsteps coming up the stairs. Their bedroom door opened and an old lady walked in. My grandparents had known the previous owner well and immediately recognised the figure as her! The old woman walked up to their bed, seemed to peer at them for a few seconds, then turned round and left the room. Her footsteps could be heard as she walked down the stairs again.

My grandparents were amazed by their experience, and more so the following morning. The daughter of the old lady was found lying dead in her garden, next door. To my grandparents it seemed that the spirit of their dead friend had returned for her daughter.

Three houses in the delightful Georgian crescent in King Street, Leicester are said to be haunted, although it is not known if any of the apparitions have been seen or felt recently.

In one the haunting takes place on the landing. A door slowly opens of its own accord and the frightening figure of an old man with bushy grey hair walks out from a room onto the landing. He is described as having a malevolent expression. The fact that a man once hanged himself on the landing is naturally connected with the ghost.

Confirmation of the story was received in 1980. Another lady who once lived in the house told how she woke up one night to see the figure of the old man with a beard bending over her husband as he lay in bed. The figure disappeared as she watched in trepidation!

In another, the ghost of an old lady appears. She is seen walking along, smiling at people. A feeling of peace and serenity has been experienced by the witnesses. In the third house the haunting takes the form of an evil presence which is felt but not seen. On one particular occasion, when a children's party was in progress, the laughter and chatter suddenly stopped and the atmosphere turned icy cold. Everyone in the house said that they felt as if some terrible entity was present.

Brooksby Hall too has its own ghosts, such as a former mistress of the house, Lady Caroline, who is supposed to haunt the building. It is said that this particular story dates from the beginning of the 1890s when workmen uncovered a woman's skeleton while doing some alterations. Another tale connected with Brooksby is one which takes place at midnight, a few days before Christmas, when a coach and horses is seen thundering towards the centre of the Hall. It apparently then stops to unload a heavy object, and proceeds to thunder away into the night.

The Gardener and the Elizabethan

The Abbey of St Mary of the Meadows, Leicester, founded in 1143, is famous as the site of Cardinal Thomas Wolsey's death in 1530. Nothing now remains of the original building except for some portions of masonry which are incorporated into the reconstructed foundations now forming part of Abbey Park.

One morning in the late 1970s one of the gardeners at the Park was kneeling on the grass working near the old Abbey foundations. Hearing someone say 'Good morning', he looked up from his work to see a man dressed in Elizabethan costume standing in front of him. The man then went on to ask who was living in the house at the moment, pointing to the ruins of Cavendish House nearby. He clearly knew the house, which was built during the 1560s by Henry Hastings, Earl of Huntingdon. The gardener held a conversation with the man for several minutes until he suddenly disappeared before his eyes. Until this point the gardener thought he was talking to a man in fancy dress or an eccentric!

The gardener had never had any experience of this sort before and has always been very puzzled by it. He told me that he could not understand why it had happened to him; he did not really believe in ghosts and certainly had never wanted to see one!

Out for a Stroll

The following account was sent to me in 1977 by a local Evington inhabitant. The witness wondered if it was simply an isolated incident or if it had happened to anyone else.

'About twelve months ago at around ten thirty in the evening I was driving along Evington Road near the Golf Course, heading towards Evington village. I observed the dark silhouette — I stress the word silhouette — of a man crossing the road from right to left. I had just about thought to myself that it was a foolhardy thing to do when I realised that my headlights should have been illuminating him, but in fact they were not, although by now he was in the middle of the road; and then he just was not there! I pulled into the side of the road and got out, not a soul was about. I have heard of black holes in outer space and this was the impression made upon me, not a life-like apparition but a human shaped nothingness.

'I have often wondered if somebody has, in fact, been knocked down on this stretch of road or whether the 'Nightwalker' still uses a course which existed through a former spinney, cleared away when the road opened up.'

A similar experience happened to a driver one night near Brooksby Hall close to the Leicester to Melton Mowbray road. He was driving along a dark country road when a figure directly in front was illuminated by the car's headlights. The driver braked the car and jumped out wondering how badly injured the person was, but to his amazement he could see the figure still walking ahead until finally it disappeared into the gloom.

This is not the only strange figure which has been seen on this particular stretch of road. A figure with long hair and wearing a full length cloak was seen on the road one evening by a woman from Hoby. The event occured as she was driving from the river towards the railway line and she was most surprised to see that the figure seemed to be walking with its knees at ground level. She later discovered that at sometime the road had been raised and realised that the ghost must have been walking on the original lower surface.

Haunted Churches

For some reason churches seem to attract more sightings of ghosts than any other sort of building. The following stories concern some Leicstershire churches and include the inevitable hooded monks.

There is an old legend connected with Leicester's Cathedral of St Martins which tells of a strange, hooded ghost that haunts the churchyard. The apparition is usually seen kneeling down, with one ear held to the ground. Perhaps the ghost is listening for passers by for it is said that if one of its long arms stretches out and touches a person walking by they will be dead within the year! As far as I know there have been no recent sightings of this apparition, but perhaps no one has lived to tell the tale!

One of the city's mediaeval churches is haunted and even the vicar has admitted that he is convinced of some sort of inexplicable, unwanted presence in the church.

A few years ago two schoolgirls visited the church during their lunch break. While looking round thcy wondered what lay behind a long curtain hung across the north aisle and decided to take a look. As they drew the fabric to one side they were startled to see what appeared to be a white sheet falling down towards them. They dropped the curtain, backing away in alarm. After calming down slightly they realised they had probably seen something which they had dislodged so they took another look. To their surprise they could find nothing on the floor or hanging up behind the curtain to explain what they had seen. The experience frightened them both and one of the girls declared that she would never go into that particular church again.

On another occasion a lady was in the Sacristy cleaning some of the Church silver when she happened to glance towards the window. She could see a face looking in through the window which she described as wearing a hood and surrounded by a strange green light. At the moment she saw the face she also heard a noise at the door, as if someone was trying the latch. Dropping her work, she immediately ran outside to see if someone was playing a joke, but the whole area was deserted. Her exit only took a matter of seconds so she would have caught a practical joker in the act — if that's who it had been.

Blackfriars Hall on New Walk, Leicester, which used to be the old Holy Cross Church, is said to be haunted by a former prior, and several stories of a ghost appearing there date from the 1920s. In 1929 Elliott O'Donnell, a professional ghost hunter and author of several books about hauntings, visited Leicester and decided, upon hearing the stories, to spend a night in the church with a friend for company. O'Donnell was to be disappointed as he did not see the ghost, but his friend did.

The ghost of a priest has been seen several times in the church. On one occasion a priest was seen approaching the altar, preparatory to taking Holy Communion to a sick person. The image of the priest was recognised as Father Norbert Wylie who had been prior there at the end of World War I and was well known for his devoted care of the sick.

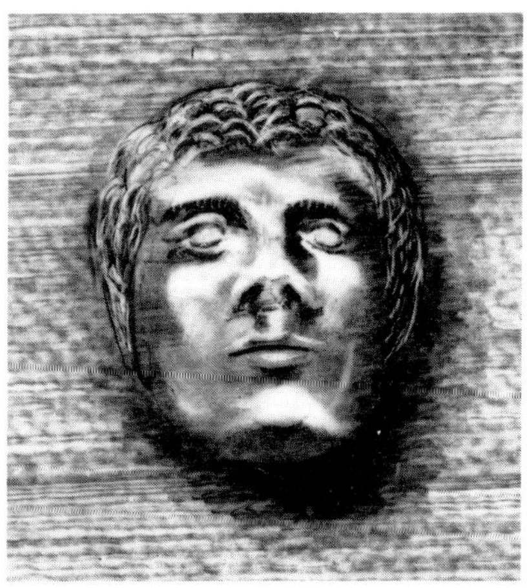

Mysterious Music

At the beginning of the century the building in Belvoir Street, Leicester which, until recently, housed the Goldsmith Music Library was owned by Sir Herbert Marshall. Sir Herbert, a well-known pianist, was the Mayor of Leicester in 1869. Under his ownership the premises were used as a music shop with a piano salon on the first floor.

Eventually the music shop together with the rest of the premises were sold. It is now many years since the salon was visited by prospective customers who would play their favourite pieces as they tried out the various pianos offered for sale. Gone too are the groups of music lovers who would gather to hear piano recitals. Mysteriously however the music lingered on and has been heard drifting down from the first floor. Nearly always the same weird tune is played. In February 1980 Mrs Louise Eggleshaw was in the building adjoining the Music Library one evening just before ten o'clock. Together with some other people she was walking down some stairs near the adjoining wall when sounds of chords being played on a piano could be heard. Everyone in the party agreed that the noise could only be coming from the Library, but upon investigation it was found to be locked up and in complete darkness.

The first floor also seems to be the scene of haunting by a ghost generally agreed to be that of Sir Herbert. Books on shelves have been known to fly out of the bookcases and drop to the floor. A few years ago one of the cleaners was working upstairs when she suddenly noticed the temperature in the room change to an icy coldness. To her great terror, this was followed by a locked door slowly opening of its own accord. The cleaner ran down stairs at this point, too frightened to stay and see what would happen next.

In 1977 an East Midlands Youth Organiser decided to spend a night by himself in a haunted building to raise funds for Help the Aged Week. The man chose to stay in the Music Library and on the evening of 8th March he was locked inside the building at seven o'clock, and was completely on his own. He had brought along a camp bed which he set up on the first floor, and settled down to await the night.

He fell asleep at about midnight after hearing lots of creaks and the usual noises a building makes when all is quiet. Somewhat later at about a quarter past three something woke him up and he heard footsteps coming towards him, then he felt a heavy weight pressing down on his camp bed, just as if someone had sat down on it beside him. 'I could not turn my head to see what was there, I was powerless until it left', he said later.

The following morning at seven o'clock the building was unlocked and the witness was let out. Reporters from the local press and radio stations were there to meet him to hear of his experiences during the night. Two radio reporters were present and recorded the same interview each on their own, separate tape recorders. Strangely, when the two recordings were played back both tapes had a blank period of about thirty seconds in the middle of the interview, each in the same place. Neither reporter could find out what had caused the blank, their recorders seemed to be working perfectly. It seems more than a coincidence that both tapes were identically effected. I have heard of several occasions, when investigators have been trying to film or record the events of a haunting, when electrical equipment being used has either broken down or refused to work for no explainable reason.

The Witness

A lady who lived in a flat in New Walk, Leicester arrived home one evening and, upon opening the front door, was disturbed to see an old man sitting in a chair near the fireplace. Wondering how someone had got into her flat, she immediately turned on the lights but found no one there. She was a little shaken by this experience as the man she thought she had seen had a beard and looked just like her grandfather who had died when she was nine. However, she assumed that it had just been a trick of the light and her imagination had been working overtime so she thought no more about it.

Later that same evening her landlady called round to see her and, according to habit, just tapped on the door and walked straight in. However to her surprise the landlady, instead of saying hello, just said 'Oh, sorry' and walked out again. The next day the landlady apologised for entering the room when she had company, only to be told that there had been no one else in the flat. After further discussion it seems that the landlady had also witnessed an old man with a beard sitting in the chair by the fire.

The Coach and the Peacocks

Lady Jane Grey is one of Leicestershire's best known historical figures. As a child she lived in the house alongside the road in Bradgate Park. Her life ended tragically and abruptly on a political scaffold in 1553 when she was only sixteen, after reigning as Queen for only nine days.

There are several stories about her ghost, which is said to haunt Bradgate. One account is that on Christmas Eve, Jane can be seen riding through the Park in a carriage drawn by four headless, black horses which then disappears as it approaches Newtown Linford Church on the outskirts of the grounds. The carriage reappears nine days later, stopping at the now ruined house, where Jane is said to get out and walk towards her former home where she vanishes again.

Another report says that the procession appears only on Christmas Eve and Lady Jane sits in the coach with her head held on her knees.

There have been other tales of strange howls and wails heard in Bradgate Park at night, but these have been easily explained by the presence of several peacocks which inhabit the ruins of the house and whose cries are particularly eerie!

The Hand on the Ceiling

Market Bosworth Hall is said to be haunted as a result of a tragedy which apparently happened several hundred years ago. The story concerns the young daughter of a previous owner of the Hall.

The daughter, Jane, used to have clandestine meetings with the son of the gardener. Her father found out and thoroughly disapproved of the affair, so decided to put an end to the meetings. He managed to sabotage the bridge which the boy used to cross in order to reach the couple's meeting place. Unfortunately, the following night the boy was late and Jane crossed the bridge in search of him. The structure collapsed and she was drowned. Jane's ghost is now thought to haunt her old room, over the entrance hall of Market Bosworth Hall. A grey shape, resembling a woman's hand, appeared on the white ceiling and, it is said, cannot be removed.

★ ★ ★

In the seventeenth century Bosworth Hall at Husbands Bosworth was owned by a Roman Catholic family. During the Civil War, mass had to be held secretly by Jesuit priests. On one such occasion mass was being celebrated in the Hall when the approach of Roundhead troops could be heard. All religious evidence was quickly swept away, and the priest secreted away in a hide hole entered from the attic. In his haste, the priest knocked over the consecrated wine. Where the spilled wine fell onto the floor, a dark stain appeared and has remained damp ever since — for 300 years.

Most later owners of the Hall were also Catholic, but in 1881 Sir Francis Fortescue-Turvile married a Protestant widow, Lady Lisgar. When one of the servants was dying, Lady Lisgar refused to let a priest into the house to administer the last rites. Because of this, it is said that she is doomed to haunt the Hall for ever. Her ghost has been seen in the past by both inhabitants and visitors, wandering along corridors and stairways. She has also been seen in the Bow Room, where she died. On one particular occasion a doctor who was visiting the house, was on his way upstairs when he was passed by a strangely dressed woman. He greeted her, but received no reply. He later asked who the strange guest was, describing her to his hosts. He was astonished to receive the reply, 'That was the ghost of Lady Lisgar'.

Castle Courtyard

The oldest part of Leicester Castle still standing is the Great Hall, built of local Dane Hill stone in about the year 1150. It is said that it was here that the first gaol was established in Leicester, possibly round about 1300. According to a nineteenth century account, the gaol may have been a vault underneath the castle with a flight of steps leading to the Great Hall where the courts were held. This romantic description of the dungeon, written in 1859 by James Thompson, goes on to tell of how trembling culprits were dragged up the stairs into the Great Hall to appear before the Earl. He would hear an account of the victim's crimes and would mete out justice, and the wrongdoer would then be hurled back down the stairs into the cold, damp dungeon, to await execution on the Castle Green. Another reference in the history books reports that the occupier of the Castle in 1634 discovered an old dungeon in which were skeletons, still fettered to the walls, indicating that the poor inmates had been left to perish in their dark abode. Modern historians no longer accept that there is much validity in these accounts, but they are certainly very entertaining.

The Castle itself is said to be haunted by John of Gaunt who inhabited the buildings during the fourteenth century, but as far as I know, his ghost has not been seen recently.

The Castle Green is also haunted, but surprisingly, not by a headless spectre resulting from an execution on this pleasant sward. The ghost which haunts the courtyard is that of a Victorian, William Napier Reeve, an historian who wrote an account of the Castle, and during his researches made many visits to the Castle area. Apparently he was very fond of this quiet spot, so fond, in fact, that his ghost continues to visit the yard. Indeed, a figure of a man dressed in Victorian clothes and wearing a top hat, was seen outside the Castle in 1981.

The Castle Gatehouse, which is now used as the judge's lodgings, may also be haunted. Some of the occupants have reported strange knocking and rapping noises which cannot be explained.

The Monk of St Bernard Abbey

Exactly 100 years after the founding of Mount St Bernard Abbey in Charnwood Forest in 1835 a strange event occured on the afternoon of 7th June, 1935 as a groom was leading two horses along the road which runs in front of the Abbey. He had just passed the Abbey gates when he saw a figure, looking like a monk dressed in a white habit, standing at the side of the road. Then, as he watched, the figure floated up the side of the stone perimeter wall of the Abbey, which is about six feet high, and silently moved along the top until it disappeared down the other side. The horses seemed terrified of the apparition and bolted. Fortunately the groom was able to catch the horses and eventually managed to calm them down, although initially they were trembling with fear. Afterwards he had very great difficulty to persuade them to pass by this portion of wall. Near the spot where the incident occured stood a small hut which housed the pumping engine for the Abbey's well, and the groom thought that the figure he had seen resembled one of the monks whom he had sometimes seen working there.

Sometime later the groom was reading an old newspaper when he came across an article reporting the death of one of the monks from the Abbey. On the very day the groom had seen the apparition a certain Brother Finbar Holland had gone to the hut to investigate why the pump was not working and had later been found dead on the steps. Sadly, the young Brother died only three days before he was due to be ordained to the priesthood by the Bishop. The Ordination cards had already been printed and his family had been invited. His relatives came, but to an unexpected funeral.

Another Pair of Hands

At half past one on a night in the early 1970s four men were on duty at a bakery in Abbey Lane, Leicester when they observed another man walking across the end of the room. They were rather surprised by this as they knew they were the only people officially in the building. Consequently, they gave chase immediately but, despite searching the entire premises, could find no one about.

The following night the men heard footsteps in the mess hall, the next room to where they were working. Once again they investigated, but could find no trace of anyone in the building.

On the third night they were in the mess hall itself when they suddenly caught sight of the shadow of a man's head moving along a wall. Following the shadow as it progressed, they watched in amazement as it disappeared through the wall.

Ghosts do not only haunt old buildings, but new ones as well. During the construction in 1978 of new business premises in Wellington Street, Leicester, a lift was being installed and, tragically, one of the workmen fell down the lift shaft and was killed. It is said that his ghost now haunts the building. Staff have heard a voice in or near the lift, and a figure has been seen walking down corridors, but disappearing round the corners.

Another haunting takes place at a Thurmaston food factory. A figure of a man dressed in a flying suit with a fur collar has been seen by staff working at the factory in the evenings.

A clairvoyant who investigated the haunting believed that the ghost was probably that of a pilot or a plane's crew member from World War II. There was a scrap yard on or near the site of the factory, and one theory is that the ghost's crashed plane was left at the site.

Soldiers from the Past

There are many strange stories from all over Britain of ancient soldiers returning to haunt their battle sites. The Battlefield of Bosworth, at Sutton Cheney, seems to have its own ghosts as well. Sightings of a ghostly horseman and a headless soldier have been reported in the area of the field. They are naturally connected with the Battle of Bosworth in 1485, between Richard III and the future King Henry VII.

Just to the south of Leicestershire lies Naseby, the site of a battle in 1645 when Charles I was defeated by Sir Thomas Fairfax and Cromwell. The following account of a strange incident which took place some years ago to a colleague of mine, and her boyfriend seems to be strongly related to this historical event. They each wrote down their own impressions of what they had seen.

The man's account read: 'Impossibly hot and humid, not a breath of wind, you could feel the stillness; even the birds made no sound. Sprawling in the grass, the hairs on the back of my neck began to bristle. Cornfield and grass were silent.

'What could have been an old drover's road suddenly became filled with figures, low wooden carts pulled by tired, dusty, weary men passed by, chains hung from the carts — what they were for I don't know. No sound from men nor carts as they moved slowly by. I suppose what really made me feel I was a witness to some bygone age was the recognition of a kind of uniform the men appeared to be wearing, not dashing Cavaliers, just impossibly exhausted men.'

The girl wrote: 'On the 14th June 1949, my boyfriend, now my husband, and myself took sandwiches and lemonade and cycled to Naseby. We pushed our bikes some way along a bridleway then sat down on the grass, leaning back against a haystack. The day was — well, peculiar is the only word — so hot and heavy that the light seemed almost purple. We kicked off our shoes, ate our sandwiches and argued lazily — me, that I should expire if we did not get a storm to clear the air; he, that he could happily manage with weather like that for ever. Then I suddenly realised that there were men looking at me. No, that is not true, they were completely ignoring me. They were walking on either side of a waggon, four men, perhaps five. The waggon was very heavy and wooden with chains looped along its sides. It was flat and oblong, just like a heavy board on wheels. They were no horses; the men must have been pushing it. They were dressed in black leather jerkins and boots, grim-faced and so weary that the perspiration had run down their faces, streaking them. They were certainly no Cavaliers with fancy plumes.

'Roundheads possibly, the dress was similar to paintings I have seen, the impression was of older men, the rearguard of an army or even local villagers. However, my main feeling was embarrassment. We seemed so frivolous, so carefree, in that sad company. We must have broken some record in regaining the public road and making our way home'.

Oddly enough it wasn't until some days later when they were told that their visit had been on the Anniversary of the Battle of Naseby, that they confessed their experiences to one another. Previously each felt that the apparition was so unbelievable the other would not believe it, and yet, in the event both had seen the same things.